Excel Formulas and Functions 2020 Basics

Step-by-Step Guide with Examples for Beginners

Adam Ramirez

Table of Contents

Introduction

In the past decade Excel became one of the most useful office and personal tools out there. While it used to be associated with office administrators, accountants, and analysts in the past, nowadays it's used by everyone. It's easy to learn and it provides us with the ability to help ourselves by analyzing the data that matters in our lives. More and more users turned to Excel for help with their personal finances, for example. Nothing beats having a spreadsheet and a chart to open your eyes and tell you where all your money goes. And this is where this step-by-step guide comes in to give you a helping hand.

You probably already know that Excel runs on mathematical formulas and functions. In fact, you probably stayed away from the program for this exact reason. After all, these tools are usually used to build calculations engines, and sophisticated data analyzes. It's true that Excel analysts have the most to gain from working with this program. However, you shouldn't feel intimidated by that. Start practicing today, even if it's going to take weeks or even months for you to become a master.

It's no secret that there are over 400 functions in excel and you need to understand what a lot of them do. But this is why you got your hands on this book. To guide you, and show you that if you learn the tools correctly, you don't even have to memorize those functions. Excel does the heavy lifting for you if you know where to look.

Every chapter in this guide is built in such a way to take you from the very foundations of Excel, all the way to working with functions and tables. So let's start learning how to become more productive and allow Excel to show us where we can improve.

Chapter 1: Getting Started

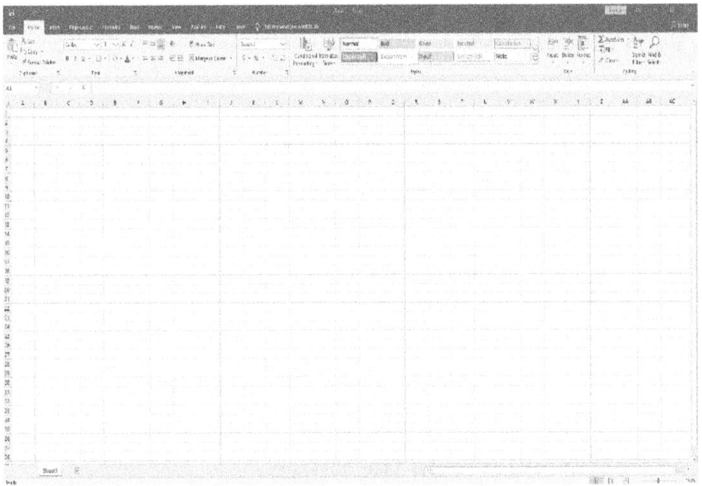

Before we start talking about complex formulas and functions, you need to start familiarizing yourself with the Excel work environment and a number of basic concepts. In this chapter you'll learn everything you need to know about the user interface and all the elements surrounding Excel workbooks.

If you've already worked a bit with Excel and you know how to find your way around the environment, you could skip this chapter. However, if you're new, or it's been a while since you last worked with this program, you should refresh your memory before continuing with the rest of the book.

Workbooks

Before we dig into the heart of the matter, you need to understand the hierarchy behind Excel. Here it is in a nutshell:

1. The Excel program
2. The workbook
3. The worksheet inside the workbook
4. A given range within the worksheet
5. The cell within the range

What we have here is called an object hierarchy. The Excel program holds the workbook objects, which in turn contain worksheets, that are made out of range objects made up from the final element, which is the humble cell. Microsoft refers to this hierarchy as the Excel object model. However, the main component we're interested in right now is the workbook. No matter what kind of operations we're performing in the program, they all take place inside the workbook.

On a side note, until the 2003 version, whenever we saved a workbook file, it had the .xls extension. Since Excel 2007, they will now be saved with an .xlsx extension. This is similar to Word 2003 having a .doc extension and the later versions having a .docx extension instead. Does the difference matter? To us, not really, unless you're trying to open a xlsx file using the pre-2007 versions, which you can't. The difference is that the xls file is a simple binary file that any Excel version can access. The newer xlsx files are compressed folders that contain all the files which hold data such as formatting, charts, and any information inside the cells.

There's no limit to how many workbooks you can create since each one is set in its own window, however, you can have only one active at a time. Sheets work the same with only one being active. You need to navigate to the bottom of the window where you see all of your sheets, and select the one you want to switch to. As an alternative you use keyboard shortcuts like Ctrl + PG UP to switch back to the previous sheet or Ctrl + PG DN to activate the next sheet.

In order to rename the sheet, you can either double-click on the sheet tab or right-click on it to bring up a menu containing various options. Furthermore, you can choose to hide the active workbook window by navigating to the view tab, followed by the window tab, and click on the "Hide" option. Take note that you can view a workbook in multiple windows, thus allowing you to see a different sheet in each window and make your work a bit easier. You can go with this option by clicking on "New Window" in the Window tab.

The worksheet we keep referring to is the most common type of sheet, which is basically like any spreadsheet you find on other applications meant to work with tabular data. With that being said, working with multiple sheets doesn't mean working with more cells, because one single sheet can contain a massive number of cells that isn't even worth worrying about. The benefit of using several sheets revolves around organization.

If you work with a single sheet, you'll end up with a lot of different data that will take a lot of time to maintain. So instead, you can have a different sheet for each type of information. You can access any sheet instantly and manipulate it however you want because you can hide various columns, change the heights and widths of the rows, choose to have several lines inside the same cell, merge cells, and much more.

Furthermore, you can also create chart sheets instead of worksheets. Their purpose is to contain a chart. However, a lot of people don't use this type of sheet because they have the option to use an embedded chart which will appear inside the sheet's drawing layer. Therefore, you don't necessarily have to use chart sheets, though it would be easier to do so because it's easier to organize them and use them for presentations.

Any version of Excel that came after Excel 2007 allows you a great deal of customization, and they all work in nearly identical ways.

The User Interface

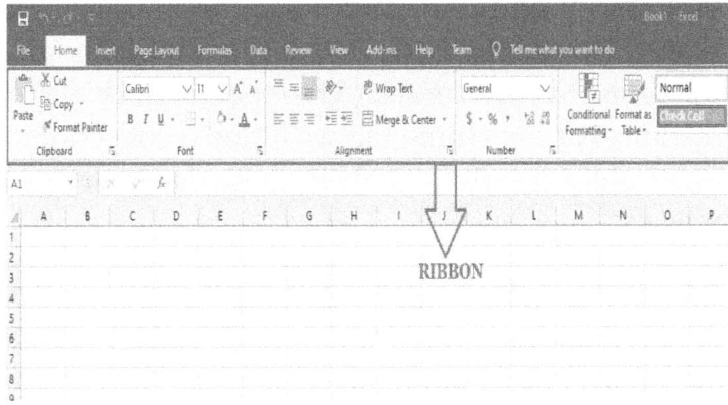

All programs have some way to communicate to the user, and that's through the user interface. Excel's UI is made up from the following components which we'll discuss in more detail:

1. The Ribbon and Tabs.
2. The Quick Access Toolbar.
3. Shortcut menus that pop up when you right-click on an object.
4. A mini toolbar.

5. A number of dialog boxes.
6. Task panes.
7. Keyboard macros/shortcuts.

The ribbon is the main UI element because it provides us with a main area where we'll find all the commands we use most frequently. This allows us to work faster. Essentially, the ribbon is a collection of tools that are spread across the program's window. It also contains several tabs that are found in all Microsoft programs, such as Insert, Home, etc. Each one of these tabs contains the tools that are connected to the category. So for instance, in the Home tab we'll find a collection of Font options, Alignment commands, and much more.

We can customize the ribbon as we wish by resizing it or collapsing various tool sets and tabs to create a minimalistic setup. If you minimize the program, the ribbon's contents will be minimized automatically, and by default the maximized window will display everything you need. Take note that the tools will always be accessible even if not readily visible. You'll just need to go through some extra steps to get to them.

Finding your way around by using the ribbon is quite easy. You select a tab and then click on the tool you need. If you really want to master Excel and work really fast, you can learn how to use keyboard shortcuts instead of mouse clicks. You can look up and memorize them, or you can hold the Alt key and hover your mouse over each tool to reveal its shortcut. Learn as you go and soon enough you'll be using more and more shortcuts, especially for those tools you use often.

For instance, if you hit Alt + HBB, you'll create a double border under whatever you selected. The Alt key is used to activate the shortcuts, then the H will select the Home tab, while the first B navigates to the Borders menu where the second B initiates the command called "Bottom Double Border." Just don't forget to hold Alt down while you type the other shortcuts, otherwise this won't work.

Next up we have the contextual tabs that are contained within the ribbon. These tabs appear only when we access them particularly as they are usually hidden until we click on a certain object, such as a chart. A perfect example for this is the Drawing Tools tab. We need to click on a shape object to enable it as it contains a number of tools and options that can only be applied to shapes.

Now, if you navigate to the bottom of the ribbon groups, you'll see a little icon that stands for the dialog box launcher. This will launch a dialog box that's linked to a particular group, like the Font group. So, the Font group icon will launch a dialog box for formatting cells if we enable the font tab.

The process is the same for other groups and dialog boxes. The Alignment group will launch the exact same dialog box as the font group, but it will enable the Alignment tab instead of the Font tab. Take note however, that you won't be using these dialog boxes often because the ribbon remembers the most often used options and tools, and therefore you'll be accessing them from the ribbon.

Another collection of tools can be found in the form of a gallery. There are multiple galleries that represent certain categories, such as the Styles gallery which lists the style name and gives us an idea about the form of our object if we select it. This type of tool is extended with the Live Preview which allows us to display the data we select and see it as it will look once we add it to the worksheet. All we need to do is hover the mouse over the chosen object. For instance, you can hover over the Format Table gallery and you'll see how the table might look like. This allows us to make a choice before fully committing to it.

Next, we have the File tab which is unique. When you click on it, you'll be taken to the Backstage View where you'll be able to perform a number of actions that are focused only on the document itself. For instance, you'll have the option to set up a new workbook, to save your files, to manage your printing, open other files, and more. In addition, the backstage view contains an Options dialog button that will launch a dialog box that contains a number of settings used to customize the Excel application.

Take note that next to all of these tabs and collections of tools we also have a number of shortcut menus that only appear once you right-click on a selected object. Therefore, these menus depend on the context. In Excel, you can pretty much right-click on any type of object and it will bring up a list of options that will only apply to it.

Finally, we have the dialog boxes that are displayed by certain ribbon commands. There you can go through various options and select other commands. Excel's dialog boxes can be divided into two different categories:

1. The modal dialog box: These boxes will have to close first before executing a chosen instruction. For instance, we have the Format Cells dialog boxes that work that way. Nothing will execute until you either click OK or the Cancel button to close the dialog box without confirming any commands.
2. The modal-less dialog box: They are the so-called "on top" dialog boxes, such as the Find and Replace option. The main difference is that they will always remain on the screen, and they're available no matter

which other activity you're performing. Its modal counterpart requires user interaction before continuing with the execution and doesn't permit us to switch to other activities unless we confirm or cancel the action.

Customization

The first collection of tools you might want to customize is the Quick Access toolbar. Normally, after the installation, this toolbar will only contain the Save, Undo, and Redo options. So, if after working a bit with Excel you realize that you're using some other commands on a routine basis, you might want to add it to the toolbar. All you need to do is right-click on the command, usually a ribbon command, and select the "Add to Quick Access Toolbar" option from the menu.

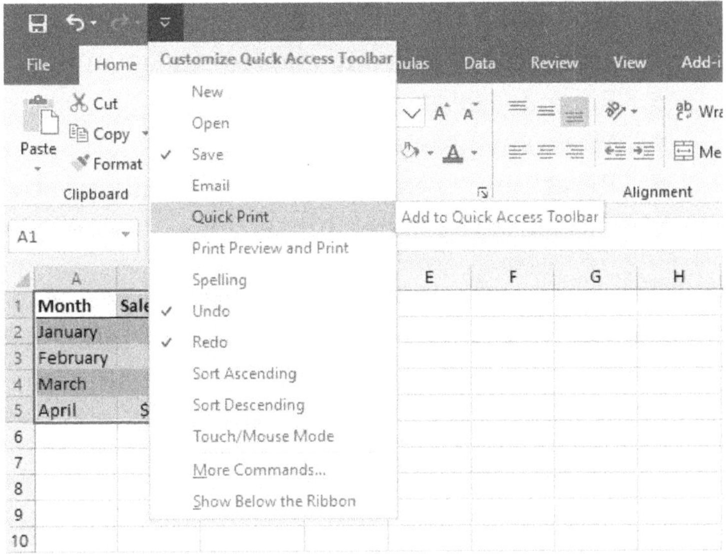

Other modifications can be made from the Options dialog box. To access it you need to right-click on the Quick Access toolbar and select the Customize option. You can customize the ribbon the same way by selecting the appropriate option in the Options dialog box. Remember that to access this dialog box you need to navigate to File and there you'll find a command called "Options."

Here are some customization options you'll have:

1. Inserting a new tab.
2. Adding a group to the tab.
3. Inserting new commands to the group.
4. Removing the commands from the group and the group from the tab.

5. Modifying the order in which the tabs are presented. The same goes for the groups.
6. Rename the groups or the tabs.
7. Move any group to another tab.
8. Reset and remove all modifications by reverting to the default settings.

While there are quite a few things you can customize, you can't remove the default tabs, the commands from the default groups, or modify the order in which those default commands appear. However, you can hide them if you'd like.

The next customizable UI component is the task pane. These elements appear depending on the type of command you issue. In essence, they're a form of response to your instructions. For instance, if you right-click on a picture, you can select the Format Picture option. As a response, the program will open the Format Picture pane. Task panes are in many ways identical to the dialog box except that they can remain visible for as long as you want and perform other tasks around them.

Normally, they will be docked on the right side of your screen, but you can move them by just clicking the title of a pane and dragging it elsewhere. Take note that this customization will be saved because Excel will remember where you placed a particular pane last, so when you open another Excel instance, the pane will be where you left it. You don't have to change its location whenever you run a new program.

Lastly, Excel allows you to modify certain onscreen elements like status bars and the ribbon. For instance, we can use the Ribbon Display options to instruct the program how to display the ribbon. We can choose to hide everything, minus the title bar for example. This way we declutter the window, which is a good thing if you're used to working with minimal user interfaces. Furthermore, we can change the status bar at the bottom by right-clicking it and choosing from a menu which type of data to display.

There are other customization options which you can explore on your own by heading to File and selecting Options. There you'll find an Advanced tab with a number of sections and commands related to customization. Try them out and forge the perfect UI.

Numeric Formatting and Stylistic Formatting

There are two more types of customizations you can choose, even though they're related to particular types of formatting, and they don't just influence the looks of the UI.

First, we have numeric formatting which determines how a value appears inside a cell. We have a default list of formats however we can also create our own by heading to the Number tab inside the Format Cells dialog box. If you can't find this dialog box, you need to select the Number group from the Home tab.

Take note that numeric formatting is applied automatically by Excel depending on the value you enter. For instance, if you add a currency sign before a value, then Excel will switch to the currency type of numeric formatting. The same thing happens if you add a percent sign in front of the value. Excel identifies the fact that you need the percent numeric formatting. Keep in mind that these formats don't alter the value you're trying to add to a cell. Even if you introduce a value with 5 decimal places and you instruct Excel to use a format with two decimal places instead, the value will stay the same when using a formula. Only the way the number is displayed will change. The actual data behind it remains no matter what.

The second type of formatting is the stylistic formatting, which alters your work purely from an aesthetic point of view. In other words, it controls the fonts, color schemes, shading and so on. You can find these commands within the Font and Styles groups that are part of the Home tab.

Finally, we can apply a number of formatting options through the use of document things. This means that we apply certain cell formatting styles, colors and fonts to the entire document, and they're all preset to look well together. If you don't feel like going through the entire fuss of customizing your document to look good stylistically, just use a theme and don't worry whether a certain color goes with another.

You can find these settings inside the Page Layout tab by clicking on the Themes group. Furthermore, you also have a conditional formatting option which means that you can instruct Excel to switch to a certain format only when a specific condition is encountered. For instance, the cells that contain percentage numbers need to turn yellow and those with negative numbers need to be red. This can be done automatically through conditional formatting.

Summary

This concludes our little introduction to the Excel work environment. Make sure to familiarize yourself with the location of the tools and options you'll be using the most, and try to customize the UI to be to your liking. The user interface of any program is like an office. The more comfortable you feel in it, the more productive you'll become.

Chapter 2: Formula Basics

In this chapter we are going to explore the basics behind working with Excel formulas. You'll learn how to enter and edit formulas, which operators to use and what they do, how to determine the cell and ranges used in formulas, and much more. This is one of the most important components in Excel, so make sure to practice along with the book and dedicate more time by working on your own before progressing to the next chapter. Take note that even though you might be familiar with mathematical formulas or you're already used to using them in order spreadsheet programs, you should still go through this chapter because there will be a trick or two, even for an expert to learn!

How to Enter a Formula

Formulas are built from five components:

1. The operator: Operators are used to write multiplication, addition, subtraction formulas and so on. You can't have a formula without them.
2. Cell reference: When you write a formula you use the cells and the ranges in order to refer to the values contained inside them. Take note that you can write a reference to

a cell inside your current worksheet, as well as any other worksheet that's either part of the current workbook, or even a different workbook.

3. Text or values: In addition to the cell data you can add your own values as well, or you can add a text string such as "weekly results." Just make sure to add the quotation marks otherwise it won't count as a string and you'll probably get an error.
4. Functions: Functions are often used to simplify your work or to write more complex formulas. For instance, you can type SUM, followed by some values inside the parentheses.
5. The parentheses: Like in math, they are used to establish an order in which certain operations are calculated.

The first rule you need to remember is that when inserting a formula in a cell, you need to start with an equal sign.

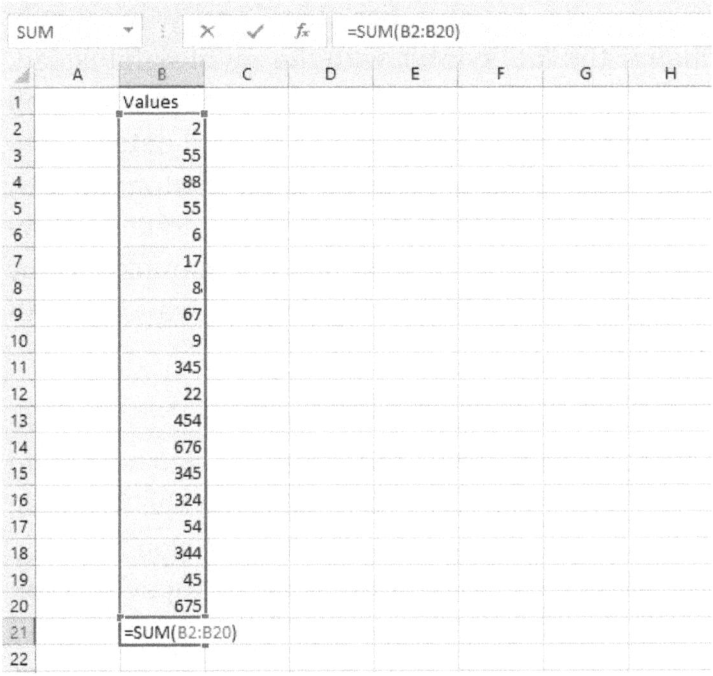

SUM | =SUM(B2:B20)

	A	B	C	D	E	F	G	H
1		Values						
2		2						
3		55						
4		88						
5		55						
6		6						
7		17						
8		8						
9		67						
10		9						
11		345						
12		22						
13		454						
14		676						
15		345						
16		324						
17		54						
18		344						
19		45						
20		675						
21		=SUM(B2:B20)						
22								

This tells Excel that you're about to write your formula. However, the new versions of Excel are a lot more forgiving and even if you don't, the program will attach a leading equal sign once you type the formula. In addition, you can also use the "at" symbol at the start of the formula because that means you're about to use a function. Either way works fine in Excel. Here's an example:

=SUM(B2:B20)

@SUM(B2:B20)

In any case, you'll notice that Excel will actually change the "at" symbol with the equal sign instead. These are just some classic rules that you can still use, because the modern versions will detect them and make the appropriate changes automatically. Furthermore, if you have a cell reference inside your formula, you can add it either manually, or by pointing to it. We are going to explore both methods.

The manual method simply means that you are going to select a cell, add the equal sign, and then write your formula. When you type the formula, everything is displayed inside the cell you're using, as well as Excel's formula bar at the top. Once you finished typing the formula, hit the Enter key to confirm it. The cell you used will now give you the result of that formula. However, when you activate that same cell, you'll see the formula you typed inside the formula bar.

The pointing method refers to typing a formula that holds a number of cell references, so you're still going to introduce some information manually, though not all of it. That's because Excel allows you to "point" to the cell you wish to refer to. Here's how this works if we want to use a simple "=B1+B2" formula:

1. First you need to move the cell pointer to the B3 cell. Now type the equal sign to start your formula.
2. If you hit the up arrow, you'll see that Excel moves a border box around the cell. By hitting the up key twice, you'll see the cell reference to B1 and it will appear in the B3 cell, which is the cell where we're typing the formula. Remember, that the formula also appears in the formula bar. And if you don't want to use keys, you can use your mouse to click on the B1 cell to make the reference to it.
3. Not use the plus sign, then point to the B2 cell, either with your mouse or by using the up arrow. The reference is now added to the formula.
4. Finally, hit the Enter key to finish the formula. Now you'll see the result inside the B3 cell, where you typed the formula. In order to check up on the formula now, you'll have to look at the formula bar while the cell is selected. You can also cancel your formula by hitting the Esc key on your keyboard or by clicking the X found near the formula bar.

You may think that the pointing method involves too many steps for no reason, but it's actually far more efficient and recommended than using the manual method. You just need to get used to it, but once you do, you'll realize you work faster that way and with fewer errors. After all, accuracy is key when working with data.

Names

Excel allows us to designate a name to any cell or range we want. This can be handy when writing certain formulas because we can type the name of the cell instead of the reference. To add the name to your formula, you'll just have to move your mouse cursor in the formula where you want it to be placed and use either of these methods:

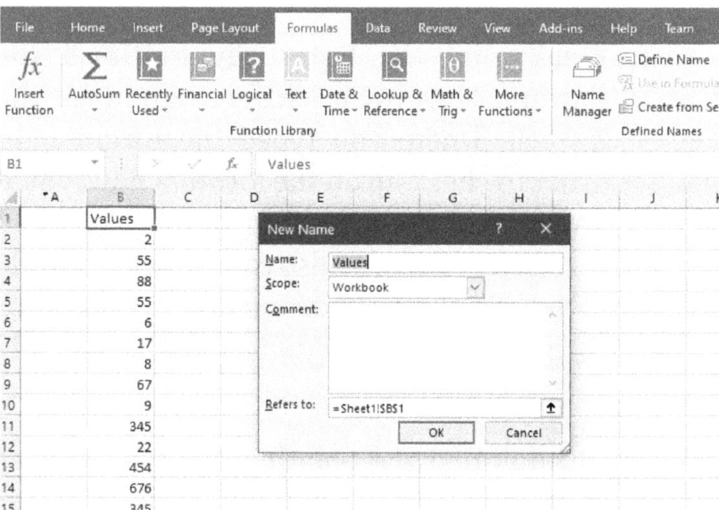

1. You can use the Auto-Complete feature when creating your formula. When you have named cells, you can type the first couple of letters and the program will start making suggestions by listing you the options that start with those letters. Take note that default functions like "SUM" are also included in this feature.
2. The second option involves pressing the F3 key in order to pop up the Paste Name dialog box. From this box you can choose the cell name you need and confirm it.

We'll discuss more about names in the next chapter. For now, this is enough for you to work with basic formulas using easy identifiers instead of default cell addresses.

Using Spaces

As you may have noticed earlier, we don't tend to use spaces when typing a formula. However, it's ok to use them, including line breaks, because they have no impact over the result. It's up to you whether you choose to use spaces. Some people prefer them because it makes the data more readable.

With that being said, if you want to add a line break within the formula you need to use the Alt + Enter keys. There's no need to worry about having too many spaces or line breaks inside a formula because you can actually insert around 8,000 characters without a problem. So, it's highly unlikely that you'll ever pass that limit even if you do use a high number of spaces.

Formula Examples

You can write any formula you can think of using the aforementioned method, as long as you have some basic math knowledge. But just in case we're going to go through a few simple formulas as examples in this section.

Let's start with a simple multiplication problem like:

=100*.01

The result is 1. Of course, this isn't a very useful example, but you will occasionally perform simple operations, or you might use Excel as a calculator instead of switching to an actual calculator application. We'll talk more about this aspect later.

Next we have a basic formula that will add the values in three cells and give us their sum:

=A1+B1+B100

Now let's use some named cells like we discussed:

=Income-Rent

This formula will subtract whatever value is in the Rent cell from the value inside the Income cell.

Next up we can use a function, like the SUM function to add all the values within a range of multiple cells:

=SUM(A1:A25)

Beats typing A1+A2+A3+...A25, doesn't it?

Now let's do something new and use the equal operator to compare the values within the cells. This kind of formula can only give us two results. The comparison can either turn out to be TRUE or FALSE:

=B2=D35

Finally, let's write a slightly more complex formula that changes the order of the operations by using parentheses:

=(A10-A15)*C3

First we subtract the value from A15 from the value within A10 and afterwards we multiply that result by the value inside the C3 cell.

Think of any other formula you'd like and try it out!

How to Edit a Formula

At some point you'll come across a situation when you need to edit your formulas. This might be due to some modifications you're making to your worksheet, or maybe you're getting some errors that require correcting. Formulas can be easily edited in a similar way you edit cells. Here are a couple of methods:

1. Simply double-click on the cell containing the formula. This automatically enables you to change the contents of the cell directly. Take note that for this to work you must have the "Double Click Allow Editing Directly in Cells" option to be ticked. It should be by default, but in case nothing happens when you double-click, head over to the Advanced tab inside the Options dialog box and check.
2. Using the F2 key. Again, this method will allow you to edit the formula inside the cell. Again make sure the option mentioned above is enabled. If it isn't however, the F2 key will switch you to the formula bar instead, and that's ok as well.
3. Finally, you can choose the cell you want to edit and then switch to the Formula bar where you can see the formula used in that

cell. Remember that cells show results after confirming the formula.

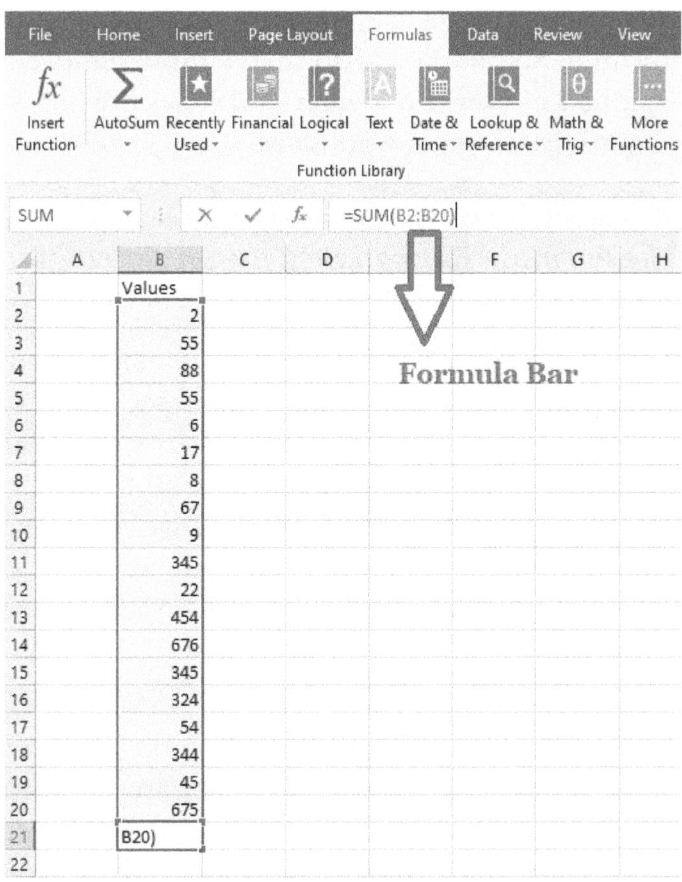

Take note that during the editing process you can select the entire formula or part of it by dragging your mouse cursor or by using your arrow keys while holding the Shift button down. Furthermore, if it's an error you're dealing with and Excel doesn't let you confirm the formula, you need to turn it into plain text and perhaps deal with it later. This might not be ideal, but sometimes it's better to move on with your work instead of being stuck with a faulty formula. So in order to do that, simply remove the equal sign. You can always add it back when you plan to figure out the problem.

The Formula Bar can Be a Handy Calculator

As mentioned earlier, if you want to make a certain calculation you don't have to use an actual calculator or open up your favorite calculator application. The formula bar can be used on its own as a calculator. So for example we are going to type the next formula into any cell we want and then store just the result:

=(110*1.01)/12

As you can see, this formula will return the same result no matter what. So, we can store that result by pressing the F2 key to edit the cell, followed by the F9 key and Enter. Now the result is stored instead of the formula. Take note that this method can be applied when working with cell references too, it doesn't have to be solid values.

However, this method is much more useful when dealing with functions instead of just basic formulas. We'll discuss functions in more detail later, but, for now, let's go through a simple example:

=SQRT(339)

Here we're trying to determine the square root of 339. Once you input the data in the cell, hit the F9 key, followed by Enter. The result will be recorded on its own. Finally, we can also just take a part of the formula and convert it into a value using the same technique. Write a formula such as the following:

=(222*1.02)/B2

Then select the multiplication operating within the parentheses and hit the F9 key followed by Enter. As a result, the formula will now look like this:

=(226.44)/B2

Formula Operators

The operators are one of the most basic elements used to write formulas and without them we can't really perform any operations. Excel offers support for a number of operators and not just the standard addition, subtraction, division, and multiplication operators we used until now. Here are the rest:

1. % This is the percent operator that technically isn't an operator under other circumstances. However, in Excel it works like one by dividing any number by a value of 100 if used inside a formula. Otherwise, it's used to represent a percent value.
2. ^ This operator represents exponentiation.
3. & This is translated as text or string concatenation. The operator is used to join strings together. For instance, the concatenation of the strings "Super" and "man" results in the text "Superman."
4. = The equal sign represents the logical comparison "equal to."
5. > Another comparison operator that means "greater than."
6. < This means "less than."
7. >= "Greater than or equal to."
8. <= "Less than or equal to."
9. <> This strange operator means "not equal to." In other programs the equivalent to this would be !=, but this isn't used in Excel.

While these are typical mathematical operators you may already be familiar with, Excel also offers support for three reference operators:

1. The colon (:) is a range operator. In other words, it creates a reference to all the cells within a certain range.
2. The comma (,) represents union. It is used to combine a number of cell or range references to create a single reference.
3. The single space represents an intersection. In other words it creates a reference to the cells that are common to two references.

Now let's see some of these operators in action by creating a number of formulas with them.

Let's start with string concatenation in order to create a new string from multiple text strings:

="Figure-"&"42A"

Remember that text strings need to be written in between quotation marks or the formula won't work. In our example we have two strings. The first one is "Figure-" and the second is "42A." By using the & operator we combine them into a single string, namely "Figure-42A." Take note that concatenation also works when used with cell references, not just actual text.

Next up we have the exponentiation operator that is used to raise a value to the specified power and produce a result. Here's a simple example:

=2^3

The result is 8 because we raised the value of 2 to the third power. However, normally you'd use cell data and not direct value calculations. So, you'd raise the value inside certain cells to the specified power.

Next we have the logical operators that can return the value of TRUE or FALSE. Here's a simple example assuming that the value in cell A2 is 10 and the value in cell B2 is 12:=A2<B2

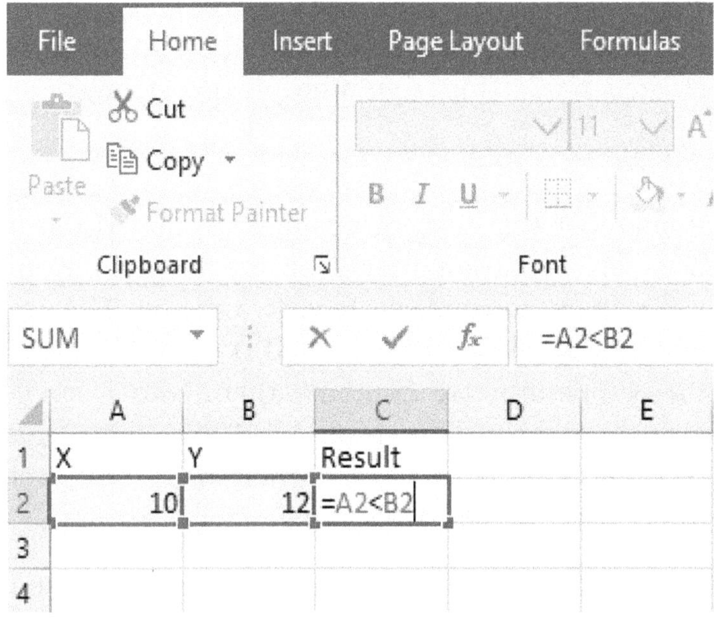

The result is TRUE because 10 is less than 12. The other logical operators work exactly the same way.

Take note that in Excel we don't have the AND and OR operators. However, you can use functions instead in order to specify them. Here's an example where the result will be true if cell B2 is equal to 10 or 12:

=OR(B2=10,B2=12)

The AND function works the same way.

As a final note on formulas, you need to know how to use nested parentheses, or in other words, parentheses within parentheses. They are needed when working with more complex formulas, and Excel processes the deepest nested operation first, followed by a hierarchical progress as it works through the operations. Here's a simple example:

=((A2*B2)+(C3*D3)+(D4*E4))*A7

Here we have four sets of parentheses where three of them are nested within the fourth. The program will go through every nested set and calculate the sum of the three results. Only at the end will the multiplication operation be performed. You can use nested parentheses as much as you want, even if you don't really need them. We can write certain operations in different ways, but by using nested parentheses we can make the formula a lot easier to read and you're more likely to avoid messing with the order of operations. Here's an example:

=A1*B1+2

As you probably know, multiplications are performed before additions, therefore we don't really need to use any parentheses. However, we should use them anyway because it will look more orderly, and we'll be able to instantly recognize the formula with a mere glance. Here's the difference:

=(A1*B2)+2

Doesn't it look better? It's up to you at end, but most people like breaking their formulas down and organizing them as much as possible.

Summary

In this chapter we discussed how formulas are used in Excel, and we explored the most commonly performed operations. Make sure to practice dozens of random formulas you can easily think of in order to remember how the operators are used. It's important to know the purpose of each operator and what kind of result it will display. Don't confuse logical operators with arithmetic operators and remember to make your formulas as readable as possible with the use of parentheses.

Chapter 3: Working with Names

Most Excel experts know about the power behind naming cells and ranges. In fact, this is standard practice because it provides us with a number of advantages over working with cell and range addresses. In this chapter we are going to explore these advantages and you'll learn how to create cell and range names, how to create names that can work across other worksheets, and so much more. Let's get started!

The Purpose of Names

In Excel, names are used as identifiers or references to various objects, such as cells, ranges, shapes, charts, among other things. As mentioned before, if you name a range you can use that name in your formulas instead of always having to use the cell references. For instance, let's say that in the range C2:C500 we have data regarding company sales. Then we have cell D1 that contains information on the sales commission rate. Here's the kind of formula where we might use this kind of data:

=SUM(C2:C500)*D1

It all looks good, but we can't really tell from a glance what's going on. We would have to go through the spreadsheet and figure out what the range is all about and what the D1 cell stands for. We can avoid all that by working with names. So, let's rewrite this formula and name the range "Sales" and the D1 cell "Commission." Here's how the formula would look like now:

=SUM(Sales)*Commission

That's much better, isn't it? We instantly know what we're trying to calculate because the formula already contains some kind of documentation regarding the values being used.

With this example in mind, here's a number of other advantages for using names instead of just cell and range references:

1. The most obvious advantage is the one we already discussed. A complex worksheet will be easier to read when using names. In addition, if other people are going to use your work they'll certainly be grateful for using names and not generic "=E27+F90." Names will also minimize human error because it's easier to type the correct descriptive name of a cell instead of its address.
2. On the left side of the Formula bar we can have a very useful Name box which we can

use to navigate through the worksheet using cell names. You'll also see the name of the cell in this box when you click on it. Use this feature to also double- check that you named the correct cell with the right name you intended.

3. Formulas are much simpler when using names, especially when you're writing a long and complex formula. This way you can also insert the cell names from the dropdown list instead of typing them, thus minimize typos/errors.
4. Once you gain some experience you'll probably want to create your own macros and shortcuts to work even more efficiently. You can create them with cell addresses, but again it's much easier to do it by using cell names instead.

Before we start getting technical about working with names, you need to understand that there are two different levels at which they can be used. First, you can have names at the workbook-level. This means that you can use the same names on all the worksheets contained within the same workbook. And secondly, we have the names only at the worksheet-level. This means that we can only use them inside the worksheet where we define them and that we can have more than one identical names at this level within the same workbook. For instance, in one workbook we might have three different worksheets and each one of them has a “total_expenses” cell, even though they aren’t connected to each other.

In most cases however, we’re going to be working with workbook-level names. There are only a few exceptions when we might use the worksheet-level names. For instance, let’s say we have a workbook in which we add a new worksheet every month to store the monthly data. We create a July worksheet and then define a number of cell names only meant for this worksheet. Afterwards, we can just copy/paste the July worksheet and rename it to August and the worksheet-level names will also be copied, but they’ll now only work for the August sheet. We’re going to talk more about these names and how to reference them properly in the next section.

Name Referencing

When you need to use a workbook-level name in any of your sheets, you need to reference it by simply using its name. When it comes to worksheet-level names, however, you need to write the name of the worksheet before the reference name. Keep in mind that you don't have to do this if you're using the name in the same sheet where you defined it.

So for example, let's say that we have a workbook that contains two worksheets called Sheet1 and Sheet3. We are going to have a workbook-level name called "Expenses", a worksheet-level name called Candle_Sales that is defined in Sheet1, and Wax_Sales which is defined in sheet two. In order to make a reference to the workbook-level name in the sheets, you just use the name as it is:

=Expenses

If you want to use the worksheet-level name that's defined on the same sheet, you use the same method by simply calling its name:

=Candle_Sales

However, if you want to use Candle_Sales on Sheet2 instead, then you need to write the reference with the sheet name. Otherwise, Sheet2 won't know where the name is coming from because it doesn't contain its definition. Here's how it works:

=Sheet2!Candle_Sales

Take note that if the name of the sheet contains spaces in between the words you'll have to use single quotes around it. So, our example would look like this if the name of the sheet is "Sheet 2" instead of Sheet2:

='Sheet 2'!Candle_Sales

Working with sheet-level names might be a bit challenging because Excel allows us to define them even when we have a workbook-level name that's identical to the sheet one we're trying to create. You need to be careful in this case because Excel isn't going to throw any errors about this process because it's a legitimate one. Names at the sheet-level simply come before the workbook-level names as long as they're used inside the sheet where they're defined. You can imagine how quickly this can cause confusion when you're dealing with a great deal of data that involves a lot of sheets and a long list of names.

In order to avoid defining cells with identical names at different levels you need to start creating your own naming convention. Naturally, there are already some widely accepted conventions out there and you don't need to reinvent the wheel. For example, you can choose to write all of your workbook related names with a "wb" prefix added to the name. You can do the same with the sheet-level names by prefixing them with "s" or "ws." This way you'll know where you want to use "wb_Expenses" or "s_Expenses."

Naming Rules and Recommendations

Even though Excel allows you to do almost everything you want with names, it still has some rules that you must follow. There are also a number of recommendations that you should probably follow if you're going to work with others who are very likely to follow the same standard. Here are some of the most important ones:

1. You may have noticed that in cell names we never used spaces. That's because Excel doesn't allow us to. Most people will use the underscore to simulate the space, but there are some who choose the period instead. Use whatever looks better to you: daily_sales or daily.sales.
2. Excel doesn't allow us to start the name with a number. It either has to be a letter or underscore sign.

3. Cell names have to be different from cell addresses. So, you can't name cell B5 to be the new Z42. However, there are some exceptions to this rule like Q3 that stands for Quarter 3 of the financial year. You can also use one letter names like X, but the entire reason for using names is to have something descriptive to represent the value.
4. The use of symbols is limited either by Excel or by typical standards followed by Excel experts. So avoid using them altogether, unless it's the underscore or period symbols.
5. Names are limited to 255 characters.
6. In Excel, unlike in other programs, the names aren't case-sensitive. This means that TotalExpenses is the same as totalexpenses. Capitalization isn't considered when defining the names or using them in formulas.

While these rules and guidelines should be followed by every Excel user, there are some exceptions where they don't apply. For instance, you know that you can use periods, however, you can't use them in the event you are constructing a name that looks exactly like a range address. So for instance X1.X10 is identical to the X1:X10 range address. But this shouldn't be a problem because you shouldn't be using any names that resemble addresses anyway because that defeats the entire purpose of using them.

The other exception is regarding a list of names that Excel reserves for its own internal use. If you really want to, you can override them, but you really shouldn't. Just try to avoid obvious names such as Sheet_Title, Database, Extract, Print_Area, and Print_Titles.

Using the Name Manager

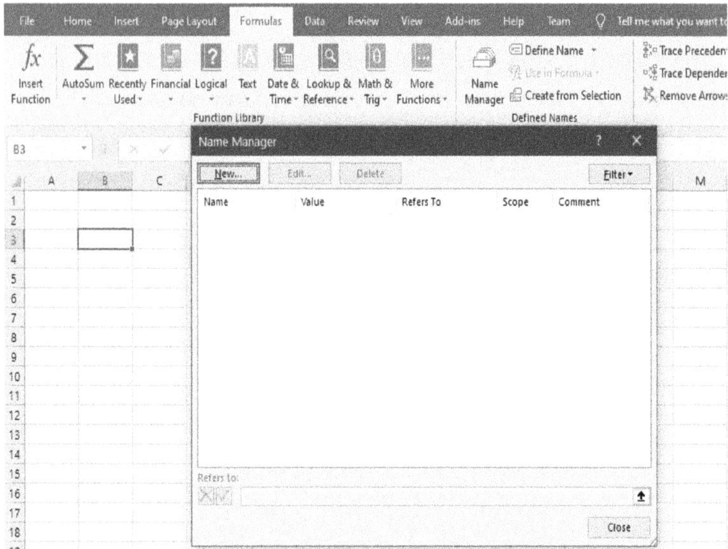

Now you can get started and work with more complex worksheets and formulas by using names. However, maintaining them may not be that easy when your projects grow to serious proportions. That's why you need to learn how to use the name manager.

Chances are that by default the name manager isn't displayed in your Excel version, so head over to the Formulas tab, followed by clicking on the Defined Names and there you'll find the Name Manager. A dialog box will open and you'll see all the names you already created. You can edit or delete them, or you can create new ones from the manager.

In the main tab you should see the value that's attached to the name, what that name represents, and the comments you may have written in order to describe the purpose of the name. You can see the names however you want in this window because you can even use a number of filters. That way you don't have to scroll through hundreds of them to find that one specific element you're interested in.

To create a new name using the name manager you'll see a button called "New." Press it and it will open a new dialog box where you can create the name, define it, and add its references. In addition, you'll be able to write a comment. This is useful because you might forget the purpose of the name at some point. Or maybe you work with other teammates on the same document, so they need a better idea about what you're talking about. If you're linking a range address to the name, you'll have to use the "Refers To" field.

If you need to edit a name, you have the Edit button in the main window of the name manager, which will open the Edit dialog box. You'll see that it looks the same as the new name dialog box because you're basically changing the same kind of information. The only thing you can't change by editing is the scope of the name. However, this isn't the only editing method you can use. For instance, you might not even have to open the Edit dialog box if you want to change only the Refers To element because you can find that option in the main panel when you open the manager itself. Just choose the name you need to edit and make your changes to the Refers To section.

Finally, you can use the name manager to delete the names you no longer need. Just keep in mind that this action is permanent and Excel will warn you about it.

Using the Name Box

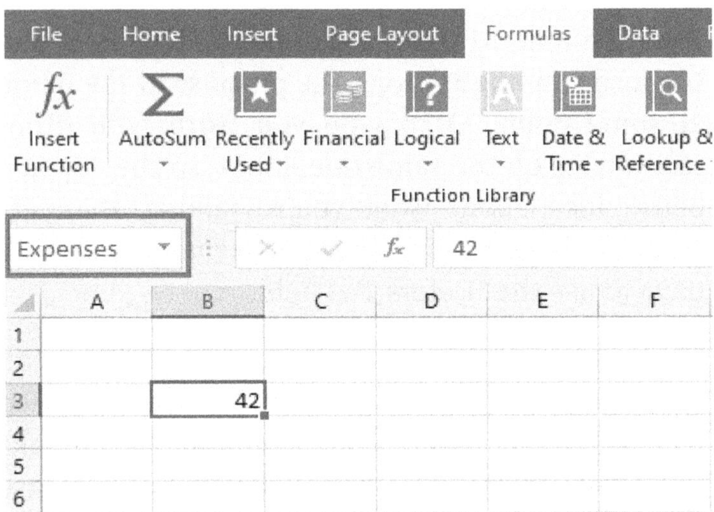

If the name manager isn't quite fast enough for you, you can use the Name Box instead to create your cell and range names. This component of

Excel is basically a dropdown list that you'll find next to the formula bar. Just choose the cell you want to name, click on the box, type the appropriate name, and hit the Enter key. Done! However, if the program detects that you already have that name, you'll have to use the name manager in order to modify the reference.

In order to create a sheet-level name through the name box, we have to add the name of the worksheet as a prefix of the name, followed by an exclamation mark. Here's an example for our Sheet1 worksheet:

Sheet1!Expenses

Same as before, if we have spaces in the name of the sheet, then we need to declare the sheet inside single quotation marks.

Take note that the name box can only be used with the already selected range. If you type a sheet name that belongs to any sheet outside of your active sheet, you'll get an error.

The purpose of the name box is to allow you to activate a named range or cell quickly. In order to select either of them, all you need to do is click on the name box and pick your name. That will select whatever range or cell you want to activate.

Name Columns and Rows

In a lot of cases you'll definitely want to give a name to the whole column or row in order to describe the purpose of the collection of values. You'll often work with spreadsheets that you need to frequently update. In that case giving a name to the cell value or range value doesn't make much sense because the next day you'll have to change the reference. That can be very time-consuming and confusing. That's when you should give a name to the entire column or row and then you just add more values to the cells below as needed, because you know what the data represents. Here's an example of a sheet called "Sales" that will represent a company's daily sales:

Month	Units Sold	Running Total
05/01/2020	20	20
05/02/2020	5	25
05/03/2020	19	44
05/04/2020	34	74

This is how Excel is used for personal reasons very often. You don't have to become an Excel master to start recording your household budget and expenses to better track and manage your personal finances.

All you need to do is define the name of the column by clicking on the letter which represents it at the top. Then you'll use the name box to give the column a name. That's it! And once you named your column you can also use it in a formula. For instance, you might want Excel to automatically calculate all the sales with the help of the SUM function.

To define a name for an entire column, select the column by clicking the column letter. Then type the name in the Name box and press Enter (or use the New Name dialog box to create the name).

After defining the name, you can use it in a formula. The following formula, for example, returns the sum of all values in column I:

=SUM(DailySales)

Summary

In this chapter we discussed the power of using names instead of cell and range addresses. As a beginner you may be tempted to continue working with the default cell references, however, you'll quickly realize how fast a document can become confusing when all you have to look at is numbers and letters that don't really tell you much. So start getting used to working with names as soon as possible. They're descriptive, and they immediately tell the user what's what. Not to mention, formulas will no longer feel like boring math since you can clearly see that you are adding the value of your house bills to the total of your expenses and not just A3+B5.

Chapter 4: Worksheet Functions

In this chapter we are going to discuss the importance of adding functions to your formulas. You'll explore all the types of arguments supported by these functions and how to use them in your formulas. Without learning the basics of working with functions you can't progress in Excel. So focus on learning and practicing this topic, because it's

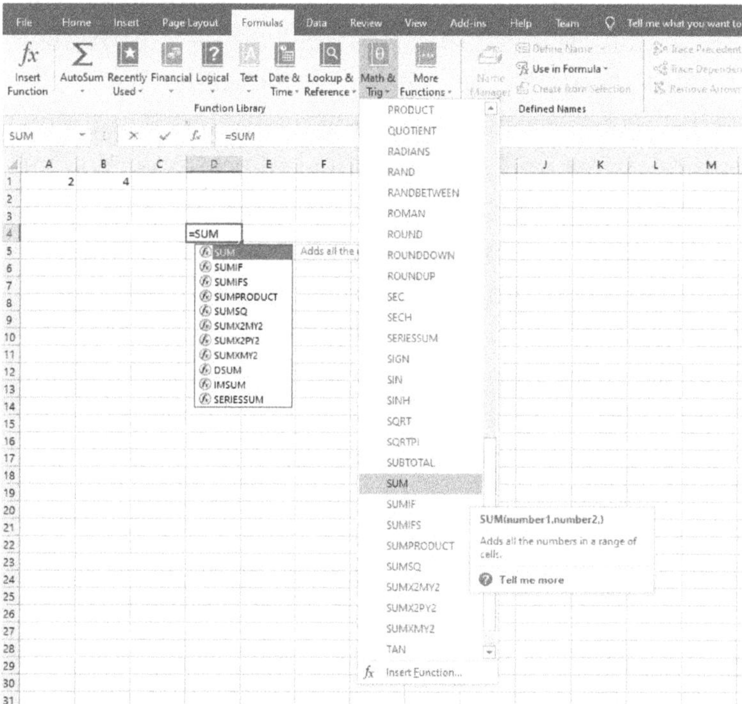

absolutely necessary if you want one day to become a formula master.

What Are Functions?

Functions are tools that simplify formulas. Not only that, but a great deal of complex formulas would actually be nearly impossible to write without functions. They allow us to make complex calculations and mathematical operations. You've already worked with a couple of basic functions like SUM, and you saw how it takes two values or more and then returns the sum of those values. Simple and efficient. The same function can accept any number of values within a range as well. With that being said, here's all the benefits and advantages of working with functions early on:

1. Keep your formulas as simple and readable as possible.
2. Perform calculations that would be very difficult without the use of functions.
3. Improve some of your editing skills, because functions are simple and faster to write.
4. Give your formulas the power to think. Functions allow you to create conditional formulas that only yield a result if all conditions are met.

Here's an example of how much simpler a formula can become by adding a function. Let's say we need to determine the average of 16 different values. If we do it the super basic way without using any functions, the formula would look like this:

=(A1+A2+A3+A4+A5+A6+A7+A8+A9+A10+A11 +A12+A13+A14+A15+A16)/16

That's one long, hard to read line, isn't it? Now imagine adding later a new row inside this range and you need to include the value inside it in this calculation. You would have to edit the whole thing to make the formula work and give you the correct result you need. Now, here's how easily you can avoid all of these headaches by using a function:

=AVERAGE(A1:A16)

Isn't that much better? It's so easy you don't even need to know any math. A lot of people are casual Excel users, and they don't remember much of their school math because they don't use it on a daily basis. So many don't even remember how to calculate the average or median value. If you don't really remember either, no problem, because as you can see, functions are basically power-words that do what they say they do. Maybe now you need to determine which value is largest and you need to go through hundreds of values. How would you do that with a mathematical formula? Doesn't matter, because you can just use the MAX function which already tells you what it's used for:

=MAX (A1:F100)

As mentioned, functions can also simplify your editing process because it removes the need to manually edit in a lot of situations. For instance, let's say we have a sheet with 10,000 names, stored in the range C1:C10000 and all of them are written entirely in uppercase. Your employer now tells you that you have to attach the names to a letter and you can't use them in their current form because all uppercase names aren't allowed. So, JOHN SMITH now has become John Smith. Since you have 10,000 names to deal with, you don't want to spend an entire week manually editing and rewriting. Fortunately, you can use a formula for this situation and say goodbye to manual editing:

=PROPER(C1)

Introduce this formula to cell D1 next and then copy it for the next 9,999 rows that follow. Next, select the range D1:D10000 and navigate to Home > Clipboard > Copy to make a copy of that range. Alternatively, you can use the Ctrl + C shortcut to make the copy. Now, select cell C1 and paste those values in with Ctrl + V or by navigating to the clipboard again. This will convert the formula to the value and you can delete the D column because you no longer need it. You have just edited 10,000 names in a minute instead of a week. That's only an example why functions are so powerful.

As mentioned, you can also give your formulas some limited form of decision-making. This is done with the use of the IF function. Let's say we have a business where the employees earn a commission on top of their regular wages. So, if a salesman sells a $50,000 item, he'll earn a rate of 7%. If the value of the products is below that, the rate is 4%. Now, if you don't want to use the IF function, you need to write not one but two formulas to determine the two values. However, with the IF function, you allow the formula to decide which calculation is the right one depending on the value of the sale which is stored inside a cell. Here's how this function would look like:

=IF(A1<50000,A1*4%,A1*7%)

As you can see, we have three arguments in the formula and each one is separated by the use of commas. They are the function's inputs and the formula is thus allowed to make a choice. The formula basically means that if the value in the A1 cell is smaller than 50,000, then it will calculate that value multiplied by 4%. If the value is above 50,000, it's going to return the value multiplied by 7%. Simple and logical. Remember that when it comes to Excel, and other aspects in life, you should work smart not hard.

Function Arguments

You may have noticed that all functions we've used so far comes with a set of parentheses containing some kind of information. That information is known as arguments. A function can be written without any arguments, with a specific number of arguments, any number of arguments, or with a set of optional arguments. For instance, we have the RAND function that gives us a random number between 0 and 1 as a result. Therefore, it doesn't require arguments. However, even in this case we still have to add the parentheses or otherwise the function isn't valid. So, our RAND function is used like this:

=RAND()

When we have multiple arguments, which usually is the case, we will separate them by using a comma in between each argument. So for instance, when using the LARGE function to return the highest value within a range we need to use two arguments. One is for the range and the other is for the "n" value. Here's how this function looks like when we tell it to find the second highest value in the range:

=LARGE(A1:A300,2)

Name Arguments

Functions require cell and range references as arguments in order to return a value. When the formula is being calculated, the contents in those cells are used to determine the result. The SUM function for instance, returns the sum of all of its arguments.

So far, we've always used cell references or ranges to calculate their sum. However, functions also allow us to use names for arguments. So, the formula SUM(A1:A20) can become SUM(Expenses) instead, thus making it simpler and easier to read.

Literal Arguments

Next, we can have literal arguments instead of names or references. This type of argument represents a direct value or string and not a cell reference. The perfect example is the SQRT function, which is used to determine the square root of a given value. It takes only one argument, and while that argument can be a name or cell address, it can also be a literal value like in this example:

=SQRT(345)

Using literal arguments isn't very common because they yield a static value that never changes. So, this kind makes the formula useless, with some minor exceptions. First, you might want to use Excel as a calculator to figure out the square root and then add in the result of the calculation into the cell. Secondly, you might want to show other people working with you that the value in this cell comes from the square root of 345 and it's not just a random value you threw in.

However, this type of argument can be more useful when there are more than one. For instance, when using the LEFT function we need two arguments to return the characters from the start of the first argument. The second argument is used to tell the formula how many characters we want. So if the A1 cell contains the name Samuel, we can return the first three letters in another cell, like this:

=LEFT(A1,3)

Now the result is Sam.

Expression Arguments

Next up, we can use expressions in our functions. What's an expression you ask? Essentially, it's a formula. This means that we can use formulas inside other formulas, except that we don't need to add a second equal sign. So, when Excel has to handle an expression inside the function, it will calculate it and the resulting value will be used by the function. Here's a simple example using the SQRT function once again:

=SQRT((A1^3)+(A2^3))

The sole argument here is the expression (A1^3)+(A2^3). When this formula is processed, the expression is first evaluated and then Excel will calculate the square root of the argument's value.

Take note that because functions allow the use of expressions, we can also add functions to those expressions. This means we can have functions, inside functions, inside functions, and so on. In Excel, we call these functions nested functions. The program will first evaluate the deepest function and then work its way out. Here's how it works:

=SIN(RADIANS(F5))

The purpose of the RADIANS function is to turn degrees into radians which are used by the trigonometric functions, such as SIN. Therefore, if we have an angle measured in degrees inside the F5 cell, the function is going to change that value to radians first. Only then will the SIN function calculate the sine of the angle, which is now in radians units. There's no concern about the limit to how many nested functions you can add. Actually,

Excel allows us to have 64 such functions inside functions, but realistically it's impossible to actually create such a formula because it wouldn't have any real world use.

Entering Functions in a Formula

In Excel, you can add the function to a formula by simply typing it, or by using the Function Library commands. A third option would be using the Insert Function dialog box, so feel free to explore all three to learn which one is the most suitable for you because they all have advantages and disadvantages.

Manual typing is the easiest method, or so you would think. The problem here is that you already need to know the function by heart, what it does and how to spell it correctly, as well as what arguments it needs to have. This method is indeed efficient and fast, but you need to memorize the functions you need.

Fortunately, Excel also comes with an auto-complete feature for your formulas.

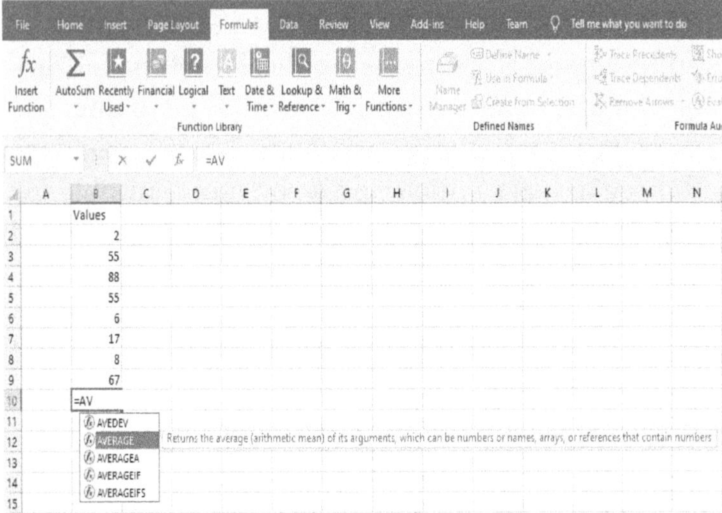

So, when you type the first letter of the function inside the cell, you'll see a drop-down list popping up, showing you all the functions that start with that letter. Furthermore, this list will come with a "ScreenTip" window that will describe what the function does. The more you type, the more you're going to sift through the list. Once you select the function, all you need to do is hit the Tab key. Now, Excel is going to open a new ScreenTip window that will tell you what arguments need to go into the function. Take note that the arguments that appear in square brackets aren't obligatory. In addition, each one of them comes with a hyperlink which you can click on and then it will select the argument for you.

If you decide that you're not a fan of AutoComplete (we all know what happens on phones and when writing text messages and emails), you are free to disable it from the Options panel. Just navigate to the Formulas window and uncheck the AutoComplete option.

If you aren't very familiar with the functions yet however, you should probably use the Function Library which you can find in the Formulas tab. Here are the categories you'll find:

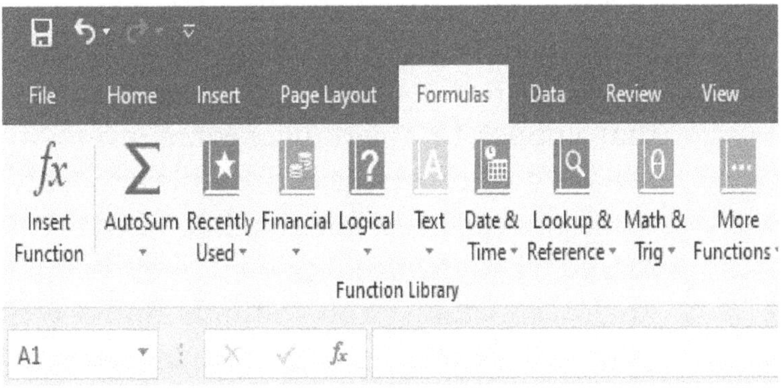

1. Financial functions: These functions are focused on performing the typical operations used when working with money. For instance, if you need to figure out how much you need to pay every month for a car

loan you might receive you can use the PMT function. As arguments, you'll have to add the value of the loan, the interest rate, and the term.

2. Date and Time: We often have to work with time frames so this is where the date and time category comes in. In this section you'll find functions like the TODAY function, which allows you to store the present date.
3. Math and Trigonometry: As the name of the category suggests, this is where you'll find all the mathematical functions.
4. Lookup and Reference functions: These functions are needed when you have to find certain values that were stored in a table or a list. Imagine having to deal with a tax table from which you need to extract the tax rate that applies to a certain income level. No need to go through the entire table manually when you can use a function like VLOOKUP to find what you need.
5. Logical functions: You will only find seven functions here that are used to test any condition. The results they returned are either TRUE or FALSE. The most useful function is probably the IF function and you already saw why.
6. Statistical functions: They are used for statistical analysis when you have to analyze a great deal of information. Here you'll find

functions used to calculate the deviation, variance, mean, and so on.

7. Text: If you need to perform some operations involving strings, you'll need text functions. For instance, you might need to pull out a number of characters inside a string, or convert the text from uppercase to lower case.
8. Information functions: This is a category that can help you to figure out what kind of values you're dealing with. For instance, you can use the ISTEXT function to see whether your cell data contains any text. Or you can go with the CELL function to learn certain information about the cell you're targeting.
9. Engineering: Excel also comes equipped with a set of functions used in engineering. This means you can work with complex mathematical operations and covert in between various measurement systems.
10. Web functions: There should be only three functions here that are used only when dealing with web address encoding and web service parsing. You'll probably not have to deal with these functions unless your work is in this niche.
11. Compatibility: Finally, we have a series of compatibility functions that are in reality some of the older statistical functions. The statistical category contains the newer and

improved versions of these functions. But due to the different versions of Excel, we have this category in case we need to handle the old versions of the functions.

This is probably the best way for now to pick your functions because whenever you choose one from these preset categories, Excel will also open a dialog box that shows you what kind of arguments you need to add.

Useful Tips

Before we finish off with this chapter, there are a few more tips and tricks you should be aware of when inserting functions:

1. If you still aren't sure what a function does, you can click on the Help button on the "This Function" link. This is probably the most useful tool for a beginner.

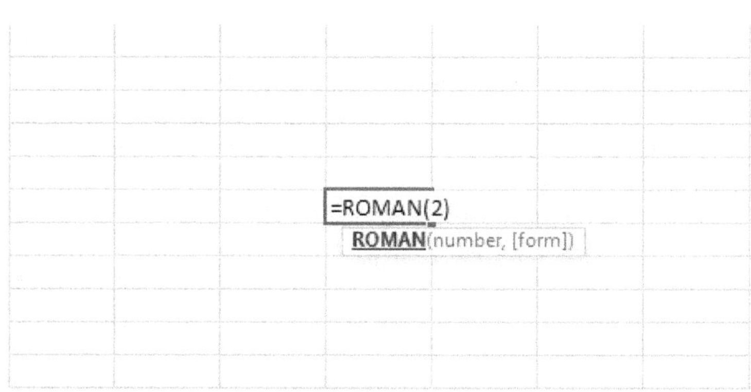

The link will lead you to Microsoft's documentation page where the function's syntax and usage is described.

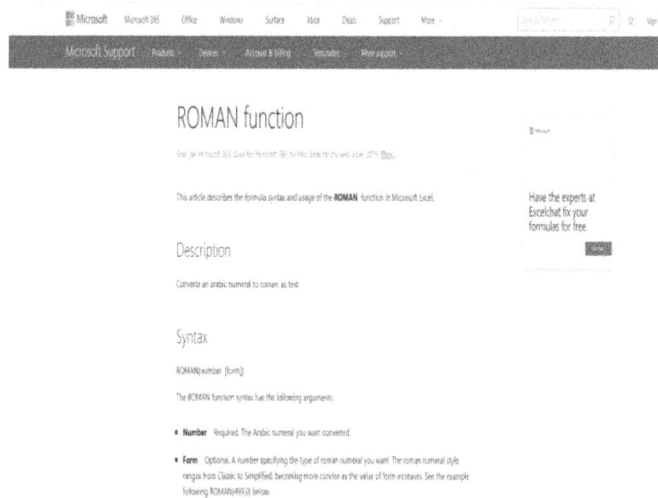

2. When you already have a formula with a function inside the selected cell, you can

click on the Insert Function button to see the arguments dialog box.

3. In the insert function dialog box you can also insert a new function in an already defined formula. All you need to do is edit the formula and add the new function wherever you want. To trigger this dialog box, simply select the function.
4. The number of boxes that appear inside the arguments dialog box depends on how many arguments the selected function uses. Therefore, if you have a function with a variable number of arguments, such as AVERAGE, then a new box is added when you introduce a new argument.
5. Next to the argument boxes you will also notice the value that was assigned to every argument. In some cases, you will see the type instead of the value; for instance, when you're dealing with text.
6. Some functions don't always have the same form. So for example, when you use a function like INDEX, you'll have a "Select Arguments" dialog box that pushes you to select the form of the function depending on what you need.
7. When you need to use the Function Name list you might have trouble finding exactly what you're looking for. First, you can use the category system here as well to filter out

the functions you know you don't need. Furthermore, remember that you can also type the first letter or letters of the function if you vaguely remember its name.

8. If you need to edit a formula that contains several functions, you can use the Arguments dialog box to focus on each individual function. In addition, you can switch to the Formula bar, select the function that needs to be changed, and then choose "Insert Function."
9. Finally, there are a number of functions that are referred to as "volatile." What does this mean? These functions will perform a new calculation if the entire workbook is being reprocessed. This happens even when the formula has a function that has nothing to do with this recalculation process. If you meet someone who's worried about using these functions, don't listen to their concerns because a lot of such functions are necessary, and we can't work without them forever. These functions include RAND, TODAY, and NOW. There are, however, some effects caused by them, such as Excel asking you to save the workbook even though you changed nothing from the last save.

Summary

In this chapter we discussed the proper methods of working with functions and their arguments. We didn't go through all the functions, of course, because Excel has more than 400 of them and, on top of that, you can create your own. We won't dive into this because you're still a beginner. But, there's no real limit to functions and that's why you can even find collections of custom functions for sale and you can add them to your program. With that being said, you shouldn't feel too overwhelmed by all of this because in reality you'll rarely need more than 20 functions. Some of them are highly specialized or not all that useful. What's important for you at this stage is to master the tools, know how to use functions, and where you can find what you need and apply it to your next project.

Chapter 5: Tables and Lists

Now that you know how to work with formulas and function it's time to explore Excel's table feature and learn about tables and lists. In this chapter we are going to focus on creating and sorting through tables, as well as working with formulas inside them.

Terminology

Before we get started, we need to lift the cloud of confusion that Microsoft dropped on all beginners who started working with Excel in the past decade. Lists appeared for the first time in Excel 2003, which back then it meant that we could work with sheet databases. Excel 2007 changed all that by turning the lists feature into the tables feature. Then came Excel 2010 which further modified the tables feature. On top of all that, Excel also has something known as data tables and this has nothing in common with the tables we're talking about. Furthermore, we also have pivot tables that are tables despite the name, and they're built by using a table. Confused yet? Let's discuss what the terms lists and tables really mean.

In Excel, a list is a set of data that's stored inside a range of cells. It contains a row of headers where we type descriptive texts, and then we have any number of rows that holds values or other types of data. So far, we've actually been working with lists to some degree.

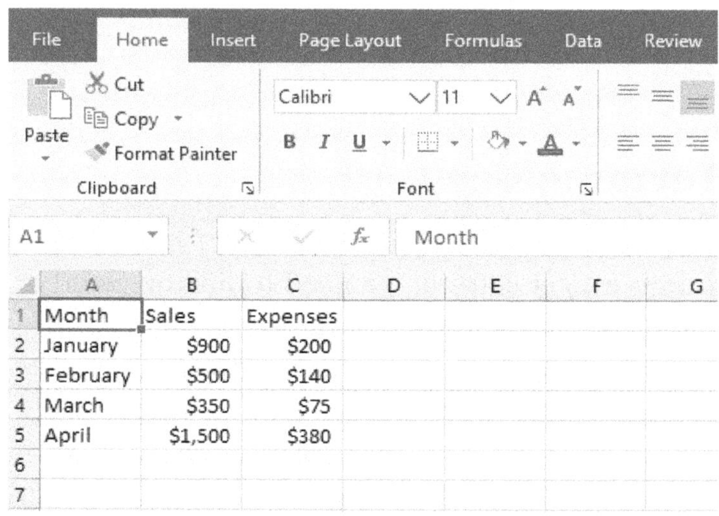

A table on the other hand is just a list that we convert to a type of range. This is done by navigating to Insert > Tables and then clicking on the Table option. This conversion comes with certain advantages, and we'll discuss them in the following sections.

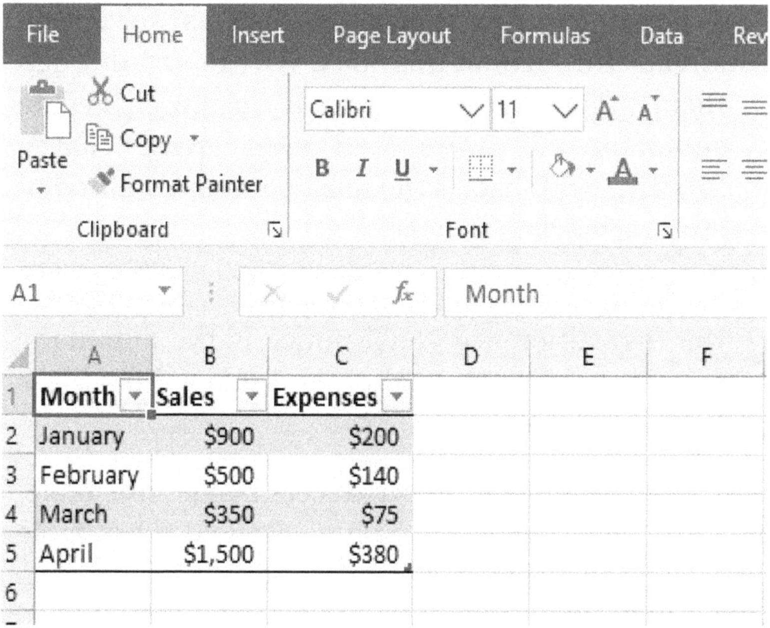
File
Home
Insert
Page Layout
Formulas
Data
Cut
Copy
Paste
Format Painter
Clipboard
Calibri
11
B I U
Font
A1
Month
A B C D E F
Month Sales Expenses
January $900 $200
February $500 $140
March $350 $75
April $1,500 $380

List vs Table

The simplest example of a list would be one that contains information on all the employees of a company. We would have a header row with the descriptive data, a number of columns, and a few rows containing the actual data. We'll have dates, numbers, text, and even logical values. We might use these lists to calculate or keep track of all the employees' salaries and bonuses.

You can do many things with lists as we've seen already throughout this book. We can sort through them, filter the information inside, calculate subtotals, edit rows, and even create charts. Working with lists is the most common method of structuring data in Excel.

Tables are nearly identical to lists in terms of looks; the first difference you'll notice is the automatic formatting. However, there are other differences that aren't so obvious:

1. When you select a cell inside the table, you're going to gain access to a set of table tools that only appear when working in a table.
2. You can summarize everything that's in a column at the bottom of the table by using automatic summary formulas.
3. The table is named automatically, and the ranges will also adjust themselves automatically when you introduce new rows to the table. The name can be edited by heading to the name manager.
4. Excel can automatically color-code the table rows and cells if you choose to enable this feature. You can find in-table styles, which are connected with the theme of the workbook.
5. The table column headers have a special filter button that you can click and you'll get

a number of data filtering options. You can sort or filter your table values this way.

6. When you scroll beyond the header row, meaning you can't see the table header anymore, the letters that represent the columns will be replaced by those header labels. So, basically, the table will free the top-level column row to show you what it represents at all times.
7. A table column will apply one cell formula to every other cell inside the column.
8. Creating charts in tables is perhaps easier, as well, because when you insert new information, the chart will expand on its own with no editing required.
9. Formulas work with table and column names.
10. Tables have an option to automatically delete duplicate rows. This feature is also available for lists but only if you navigate to Data > Data Tools and click on Remove Duplicates.
11. Selecting an entire column or row is a bit simpler and more user-friendly in a table.
12. Tables can be extended using the mouse by clicking on the lower right corner of the last cell and then dragging the entire table vertically for rows and horizontally for columns.

Now that you can tell the difference between a table and a list, let's see how we can work with tables.

Using Tables

Working with tables is indeed different and you'll need some time to adjust, however, you'll realize after some practice that there are more advantages involved than when working with simple lists.

To create a table you can use an empty range, however, in real world cases you'd be creating tables from already existing collections of data, aka lists. Here's how to create one under the assumption that you already have a list:

1. First, your data range shouldn't have any empty columns and rows.
2. Now, start by clicking on a cell inside the range and select Insert > Tables > Table. You can also press the keyboard shortcut Ctrl + T. Excel will now launch a create table window and will seek to automatically determine the range of the table, as well as whether there's a header row present. In most cases, this automatic setup will do its job. Otherwise, you need to correct its failed guesses, if there are any.
3. Click OK to confirm the table and done!

You'll now have an automatically formatted table and you'll see that Filter mode is available as well. If you go to the contextual tab, you'll also see that you have access to a new panel called Table Tools. This tab contains a variety of options that are related only to tables.

Take note that during the table creation process, the dimensions might be off if the table isn't kept separate from any other kind of data with a blank row or column at a minimum. In this case you'll have to tell Excel the precise range you're looking for. The other option is to cancel the automatic process and go back to arranging your worksheet. Then you create the table when everything is in order.

In addition, if you need to create a table from a blank range, all you need to do is choose the range and go through the regular table creation process. The table will be created and column headers will be generated automatically. Most likely they'll be named "Column1, Column2..." and you'll have to rename them manually. The formatting will be applied automatically as usual, though.

Customization

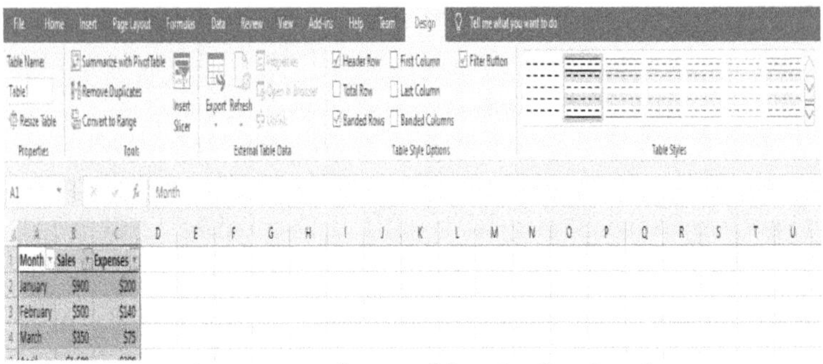

If you navigate to the Table Style Options group found in Table Tools > Design, you can make some changes to how your table looks. You can also modify what should be displayed in your table and you also have control over a number of formatting options.

Here are some brief examples of what you can change:

1. The Header: You can choose to not display the header row if you don't need it.
2. Total row: There's an option to display the total value at the bottom of the table. By default, it should be enabled, but you can disable it if you're not interested in that kind of data:
3. First column and last column: There's a different formatting style available for the first column as well as last column of the

table. Feel free to enable it or disable it, just take note that depending on theme and style you might see no difference.

4. Banded columns and rows: You have the option to display rows and columns with an alternate color, aka banded.
5. Filter: You have the option to toggle on or off the filter dropdown button that you normally find in the header row of the table.

Navigation

Navigating through the table's cells is very similar to navigating through the cells of the standard range of a list. The main difference here is that when you use the Tab key, you can move to the right of the cell you selected. In addition, when you press the same key at the last cell of the column, you'll switch to the first cell in the next row.

Another difference is that your mouse cursor will change, depending on over what you're hovering inside the table. So, you'll be able to tell when you can select the whole column for instance, because then you'll notice an arrow pointing downwards when over the top cell of the header row.

To select the entire table column you need to click twice on it. Take note that this will also select the total row and the header. You can use the Ctrl +

space bar keyboard shortcut as well, but you also need to press twice.

To select the whole row, just move your mouse cursor to the left of the cell in the first column. You'll see that the cursor will change while over that cell and it will look like an arrow pointing to the right. Click and the whole row will be selected. The keyboard shortcut for this is Shift + space.

Lastly, you might want to select the whole table. In this case, navigate with your cursor to the top left part of the top left cell. The cursor will again shift its appearance and turn into a diagonal arrow. Click and then you can drag and select all the data you want. Otherwise, you can click twice and automatically select the entire table. The shortcut for this is Ctrl + A. Use it once so you can select only part of the table data, or twice to auto-select the whole table.

As you can see the keyboard shortcuts are a lot easier and faster to use, as long as you manage to remember them. That takes a bit of practice.

Editing

When you need to insert a new column to the table, you need to select a cell inside the column that's located to the right of the table. Add some data to that cell and you'll see that Excel will automatically enlarge the table to engulf that data. The same thing happens when you add data to the row under the table. The only exception is if you add some values under the total row. In that case the table won't include that row. In this case you'll have to connect a row to a different table that has no total row, select the cell on the lower right part of the table and hit the Tab button.

In some cases however, you'll need to insert a row or a column somewhere inside the table; right-click and select the Insert option. This will open a menu that gives you the ability to insert new rows and columns.

You can also use the dragging method to simply resize the table. This is down by navigating to the low right corner of the table. Just make sure to select the table first otherwise the resize handle won't be visible. Now, move the cursor to that handle and click and drag the table to add more rows or columns.

Finally, you'll also need to delete rows and columns at some point. In this case, all you need to do is select the cell in the target row or column, right-click to open a shortcut menu, select Delete, followed by Table Rows or Table Columns.

Sorting

Tables allow us to easily sort through the rows depending on what information they contain. For instance, if we have a collection of names, you'll probably want to arrange them alphabetically. Or perhaps, you want to establish which salesmen had the highest value sales during this month. This kind of sorting is done by clicking on the dropdown arrow in the header of the column. A list of commands will open and the sorting options will depend on the type of information you're dealing with. For instance, if the column contains nothing but text, you will have two options: To sort from A to Z, or from Z to A.

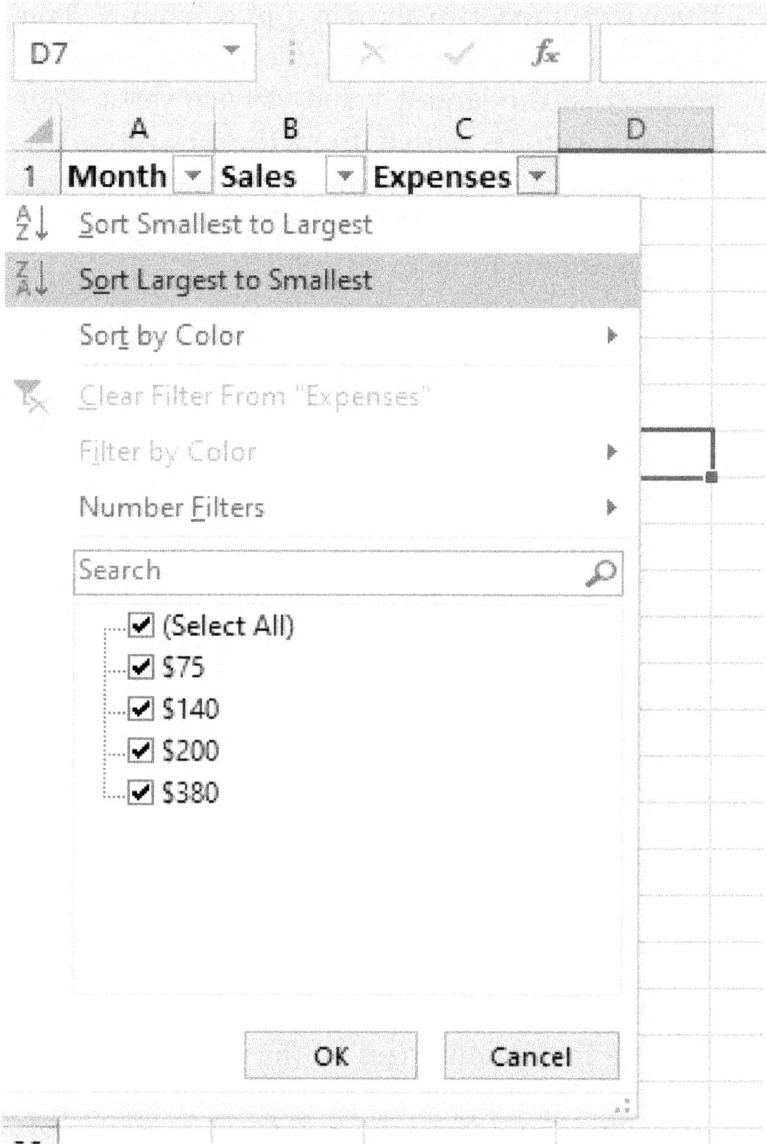
D7
A
B
C
D
1
Month
Sales
Expenses
Sort Smallest to Largest
Sort Largest to Smallest
Sort by Color
Clear Filter From "Expenses"
Filter by Color
Number Filters
Search
(Select All)
$75
$140
$200
$380
OK
Cancel

If you have numeric values in your column, or True and False values, you'll be able to sort from the smallest to the largest value, or vice versa. Date columns can be sorted from the newest to the oldest data and the other way around. Furthermore, if you color-coded your data you can sort everything by color as well.

There's no limit to sorting columns. However, the easiest way to approach a more complex table, is to start by sorting the least important column, and climb the ladder until you sorted the most valuable column last. Let's say we have a table that represents some real estate information. We can sort them based on area first, then we sort the rows by price. This isn't a rule, of course, but there are a lot of cases where your work would be a lot easier by respecting some kind of hierarchy of importance.

Using Formulas

So far, we've only mentioned the use of the Total row, which is kind of an automatically applied formula that summarizes all the values in a given column. However, in the real world we often need to work with formulas inside our table. For instance, we might need to introduce a new column that determines the difference between the present income and the projected income. This is actually an easy operation, even easier than when working with lists.

Select a cell and name it Dif. This will be the column's header. You'll also need the Present and Projected columns with some values in them if you didn't already make such a table. If you're dealing with an already existing table, add the column next to it so that it merges with your existing table. Now go to the cell under the header, type the equal sign to start a formula and then press the left arrow key. The program will now display "=[@Present]." This is the column heading within the formula bar. Type the minus symbol and hit the same arrow key twice. This is what you should see in your formula bar "=[@Presentl]-[@Projected]. Finally, hit the Enter key to confirm and finalize the formula. Excel will now automatically apply it to every row inside the table.

Take note that the formula's syntax may differ a bit if the header of the columns involve any symbols or spaces that aren't letters or numbers. If this was the case, the header text would have to be written in brackets.

Because of the possibility of dealing with syntax problems, it's recommended to allow Excel to deal with them automatically by creating the formulas through pointing. Remember, that in this example we didn't define any of these names. The formula is based on table references that are in turn based on the names. If we make any modifications to the header text, the formulas will indeed update themselves. This is another reason why working inside tables is easier and more advantageous than working with lists, even though in the beginning it might not feel like it.

In addition, our formula doesn't even have to be in the first row. This isn't a table tule. We can put it in absolutely any cell as long as it's in the same column. The table automatically fills all the cells anyway, so it doesn't matter. Furthermore, in order to edit the formula, you just need to make changes to any of the copies because the rest of them will be updated automatically.

Converting the Table to a List

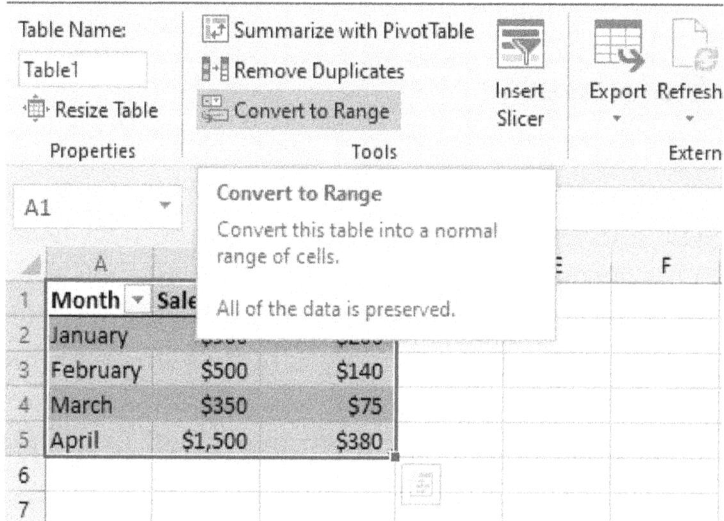

Tables are just converted lists, but sometimes we need to work the other way around and turn the table back into a list. For instance, let's say that you are working with a colleague who's using an older Excel version. In this case he might have troubles using your tables. Remember about the table feature evolution we discussed at the start of the chapter?

In order to make the conversion, simply click on any table cell, and go to Convert To Range, which is found in Table Tools > Design > Tools. That's all there is to it. The formatting won't be changed by this transformation, and the table formulas will also be converted together with all of their references.

Summary

As you progress and get used to working in Excel you'll eventually want to take it to the next level. This is where tables come. Even though they seem more complicated than lists in the beginning, they open up a way to new possibilities and in time you'll realize that you can work faster and more efficiently when using them instead of lists. Just keep practicing.

Conclusion

We live surrounded by data and information, and it's becoming more and more impossible to avoid working with it even if we aren't accountants, analysts, or working in any IT field. Over the years Excel has become the golden standard when it comes to working with spreadsheets, keeping records, and calculating all sorts of values to store them for later use.

This program isn't just for professionals or for those that have a career that involves working with any sort of data. Excel can also be used at a personal level. Start keeping track of your finances. Record your daily expenses and your weekly income. Compare this month’s finances with last month's. Create charts to see more clearly where all your money goes. Visualizing and quantifying all of this data will help you improve your life. And that’s where the purpose of this book lies. To help you do this better and faster.

So far, you’ve learned how Excel works and how to navigate through its user interface. You’ve used the most common formulas to perform a number of mathematical operations. You learned the power and functions and how to use them to make your work even easier. With the modern versions of Excel you don’t even need to memorize anything, because the program provides you with guidelines, help tools, and automated settings. Getting into Excel has never been easier than today.

So go through all the material again, practice each concept and tool, and you’ll find many uses for Excel, whether professional or otherwise.

If you receive value from my book, I will appreciate if you can leave a review on amazon.

The reason I'm asking for reviews: reader reviews are the lifeblood of any author's career. For a humble typewriter-jockey like myself, getting reviews (especially on Amazon) means I can submit my books for advertising. Which means I can actually sell a few copies from time to time - which is always a nice bonus :)

THE END

www.ingramcontent.com/pod-product-compliance
Ingram Content Group UK Ltd.
Pitfield, Milton Keynes, MK11 3LW, UK
UKHW021935190726
13853UKWH00004B/1454

9 798583 050901